K
RECIPES

compiled by
Dorothy Baldock

with vintage
postcard illustrations by
Alfred Quinton and Charles Howard

SALMON

Index

Cover pictures *front:* Cromer
back: Horning Ferry
Title page: Wroxham Bridge

Printed and Published by Dorrigo, Manchester, England. Images/Recipes J Salmon Ltd

Norfolk Dumplings

Norfolk is the county for dumplings. Dumplings made with yeast and known as "floaters" were a feature of bread-making days. In Norfolk, suet dumplings were referred to as 'sinkers', while in other parts of the country, any dumplings cooked in a casserole or stew were often known as 'swimmers'.

½ oz. fresh yeast 1 teaspoon caster sugar
½ pint warm water 2 tablespoons milk
1 lb. plain flour

Cream the yeast and sugar together. Mix the water and milk and pour over the yeast. Put the flour into a bowl, make a well in the centre and pour in the yeast liquid. Mix well, then cover and leave to rise in a warm place for 2 hours. Turn out on to a lightly floured surface and knead well. Form into 8 to 10 dumplings. Leave them to stand for 10 minutes, put into a pan of boiling water, cover and cook for *exactly* 20 minutes. Drain well and this is best served at once as a first course, accompanied by a rich onion gravy. Alternatively, though this is not traditional in Norfolk, the dumplings can be served as a dessert and eaten with melted butter and sugar.

Norfolk Dumplings should always be eaten torn apart with two forks, as cutting them will make them heavy.

Norfolk Game Stew

The English or grey partridge is the Norfolk game bird. For years in decline, today, with careful management, it is making a comeback.

Brace of partridge, cleaned and jointed   Seasoned flour   2 oz. butter
1 small onion, peeled and chopped   1 clove of garlic, peeled and crushed
½ lb. button mushrooms, wiped   4 tomatoes, skinned and halved
4 slices lean ham, chopped   Pinch dried thyme   4 cloves
6 peppercorns   Salt   Pinch of sugar   1 glass port wine
1 to 1½ pints chicken stock   A little cornflour

Dust the partridge joints with seasoned flour. Melt the butter in a large saucepan and brown the joints lightly on all sides. Add the onion, garlic, mushrooms, tomatoes, ham, thyme, salt and sugar to the pan. Combine the port with the stock and pour over. Bring to the boil, then cover and simmer very slowly for 2 hours or until the partridge joints are tender. Place the joints on a warm serving dish and keep hot. Remove the vegetables and arrange round the joints. Discard the cloves and peppercorns and skim the remaining gravy. Blend the cornflour with a little cold water and add to the gravy. Bring to the boil, stirring, until the gravy has thickened a little, then pour over the partridge joints and the vegetables. Serve the stew accompanied by triangles of hot toast. Serves 4 to 5.

Bloaters with Scrambled Eggs

A popular breakfast or supper dish in the 19th century.

4 bloaters
3 oz. butter, softened
Black pepper
2 tablespoons milk
8 eggs
Salt and black pepper
4 slices of toast

Put sufficient water into a deep frying pan as will cover the bloaters and bring to the boil. Place the bloaters in the water and bring back to the boil. Cover and simmer for 10 to 12 minutes. Drain the bloaters, allow to cool, then remove the skin and bones and mash the flesh. Combine the flesh well with 2 oz of the butter and season lightly with black pepper. Melt the remaining 1 oz butter in a saucepan. Beat the milk and eggs together, season to taste and add to the melted butter, stirring with a spoon until the egg mixture is lightly scrambled. Spread the bloater mixture on the slices of toast and top with the scrambled egg. Alternatively, the bloaters can be grilled whole until the skin is crisp, and then served with the scrambled eggs. If bloaters are unavailable, smoked mackerel make a good alternative. Serves 4.

Norfolk Beef Pudding

A suet roll filled with chopped steak and onion.

8 oz. self-raising flour
Pinch of salt
3 oz. shredded suet
1 lb. stewing steak, cut into small cubes
1 onion, peeled and chopped
Salt and black pepper
A little water or stock

In a bowl, mix the flour, salt and suet together, then mix in just sufficient cold water to form a firm dough. Turn out on to a lightly floured surface and roll into a rectangle about ¼ inch thick. Mix the steak and onion together and spread on the dough; season to taste. Sprinkle with a little water or stock, then roll up like a Swiss Roll and dampen the ends to seal. Wrap lightly in greaseproof paper or kitchen foil and then tie up in a cloth. Boil or steam in a covered saucepan for 3 to 3½ hours. Serve with boiled potatoes, carrots and a green vegetable together with thick brown gravy, served separately. Serves 4.

Norfolk Shortcakes

Not really shortcakes at all, but fruit-filled squares of pastry originally made from the scraps of pastry left over at the end of a baking session.

8 oz. shortcrust pastry | **2 oz. granulated sugar**
2 oz. butter or lard | **2 oz. sultanas**
A little milk for glazing

Set oven to 375°F or Mark 5. Roll out the pastry thinly on a floured surface. Divide the butter or lard into thirds and cover half of the pastry with dabs of one of these thirds. Mix the sugar and sultanas together and sprinkle one third of the mixture over the fat. Fold the pastry in half and roll out lightly. Repeat the process again. Finally, cover half the pastry with the remaining fat and fruit mixture, fold the pastry over, and press down lightly, but do not roll. Trim the edges and cut into 2 to 2½ inch squares. Place on a greased baking sheet and brush lightly with milk to glaze. Bake for 20 to 25 minutes or until golden. Sprinkle with a little extra sugar while still hot, if desired, and allow to cool.

Sheringham from Beeston Hill

Fish Supper

When the fishing fleets came in, housewives would go down to the harbour and purchase the broken fish not suitable for sale at the quay or fish market, using it to make a Fish Supper.

2 mackerel, cleaned and filleted   1 to 1½ lb. cod or haddock fillets
2 oz. butter   1 large onion, peeled and chopped
1 teaspoon mace   ½ teaspoon turmeric   Salt and black pepper
1 pint water
1 small dressed crab or small tin of crab meat (optional)
2 tablespoons chopped parsley
A little grated cheese

Melt the butter in a large deep frying pan or saucepan and fry the onion until soft. Add the fish, spices and seasoning, then pour the water over. Bring to the boil then simmer for 20 to 30 minutes. Lift out the fish and onion with a slotted spoon and place in a warm, ovenproof serving dish. Drain the crab meat well (if tinned), crumble and sprinkle over the fish. Stir half the parsley into the stock and pour a little over the fish. Cover with foil and keep warm in a low oven. Just before serving, sprinkle with grated cheese and flash under the grill to melt. Sprinkle over the remaining parsley and serve with boiled potatoes. Serves 4.

Norfolk Treacle Tart

This is sometimes called Walpole House Treacle Tart because of association with the Walpole family of Norfolk. Originally it was made with black treacle.

8 oz. shortcrust pastry
7 tablespoons golden syrup
Grated rind and juice of ½ lemon
½ oz. butter, melted
2 tablespoons single cream
2 medium eggs, beaten

Set oven to 350°F or Mark 4. Grease a 7 inch flan dish. Roll out the pastry on a lightly floured surface and line the dish. Warm the syrup in a saucepan until it 'thins', remove from the heat then stir in the lemon rind and juice, butter and cream. Strain the beaten egg into the mixture and combine gently. Pour into the pastry case and bake for 35 to 40 minutes or until the filling is set and lightly golden. Serve hot or cold with cream. Serves 4 to 6.

Million Pie

This is a form of Pumpkin Pie, but made with vegetable marrow. A 'Million' was a variety of marrow that was, at one time, very popular as an ingredient in jams and puddings.

8 oz. shortcrust pastry   2 oz. jam - apricot is ideal
1 lb. vegetable marrow, peeled, de-seeded and cut into small cubes
1 egg, beaten   Rind of ½ lemon and 1 teaspoon of juice
1½ tablespoons soft brown sugar   Pinch of ground nutmeg

Set oven to 400°F or Mark 6. Grease an 8 inch flan dish. Roll out the pastry and line the dish, keeping the trimmings for decoration. Spread the jam evenly over the pastry base. Boil the marrow until soft, then drain very well and leave in the pan to cool. When cold, stir in the egg, lemon rind and juice, sugar and nutmeg, and beat until smooth. Turn the mixture into the pastry case and sprinkle a little more brown sugar and nutmeg over top. Roll out the pastry trimmings, cut into strips, and decorate the pie with a 'lattice' pattern. Bake for 15 minutes then reduce oven to 350°F or Mark 4 and bake for a further 15 minutes until the pastry is golden. Serve hot or cold with custard or cream. Serves 4 to 6.

If desired 2 oz of currants or sultanas can be added to the mixture, but this is not considered to be wholly traditional.

Yarmouth Straws

A savoury version of cheese straws made with the addition of strips of kipper fillet.

4 oz. shortcrust pastry
1 to 1½ oz. strong Cheddar cheese, grated
Pinch of cayenne pepper
4 oz. kipper fillets
1 egg, beaten *(if required)*

Set oven to 375°F or Mark 5. Roll out the pastry on a floured surface to about ¼ inch thickness. Sprinkle half the grated cheese over the pastry and season with cayenne pepper. Fold the pastry into three and roll out lightly. Sprinkle on the remainder of the cheese, season with cayenne pepper, and roll out again. Cut the pastry into strips about ¼ inch wide and 3 inches long. Cut the kipper fillets into thin strips of the same length. Place a strip of kipper on a strip of pastry and twist together pinching the ends to secure. Brush lightly with a little beaten egg, if desired, and place the straws on a greased baking sheet. Bake for about 20 minutes until the pastry is golden.

Norfolk Stew with Green Dumplings

A popular festive supper dish from the 18th and 19th centuries.

**1 small, oven-ready chicken 1 lb. stewing steak, chopped
4 rashers streaky bacon, chopped 4 lambs' kidneys, skinned, cored and halved
2 large onions, peeled and sliced 1 lb. carrots, peeled and sliced
½ teaspoon ground mace 2 dessertspoons lemon juice A bouquet garni
Salt and black pepper 8 oz. button mushrooms, wiped Chopped parsley to garnish**

DUMPLINGS 8 oz. self-raising flour 3 oz. suet 4 tablespoons chopped fresh parsley

Divide the vegetables between two large saucepans. Place the chicken in one saucepan on top of half the vegetables, with half the herbs, mace, bouquet garni and lemon juice and put the steak, bacon and kidneys similarly in the second pan. Cover each with water, bring to boil and simmer for 1 hour. For the dumplings, mix the ingredients to a stiff dough with just enough water, roll into 1 inch balls with floured hands and divide between the two pans, together with the mushrooms. Cover and cook for further 30 minutes. Remove the dumplings and keep hot. Take out the chicken and remove the skin and bones, cut the meat into chunks and combine all the meat with the vegetables removed from the pans on a large serving dish and keep hot. Combine the gravy from both pans, bring back to the boil and thicken. Arrange the dumplings around the meat/vegetables and pour some gravy over; garnish with parsley. Serves 6 to 8.

Nelson Slices

Sometimes called Nelson Cake, this is a Norfolk version of Bread Pudding, named after Admiral Nelson who was a Norfolk man, born at Burnham Thorpe on the north coast, where his father was Rector.

1 lb. stale bread
3 oz. sultanas
3 oz. raisins
4 oz. brown sugar
½ teaspoon ground nutmeg
Grated rind of ½ lemon
2 tablespoons orange marmalade
3 oz. butter, melted
1 egg, beaten
1 tablespoon rum

Soak the bread in water for 1 hour. Set oven to 400°F or Mark 6. Butter a deep pie dish or roasting tin, about 7 inches x 11 inches or similar. Squeeze the water out of the bread, put it into a bowl and break up any lumps with a fork, until the bread is creamy. Stir in the dried fruit, then add the rest of the ingredients and beat well together. Turn into the dish or tin, spread out evenly and bake for 30 to 40 minutes. While still hot sprinkle with a little extra sugar. Serve sliced, hot as a pudding with custard or cream or cold as a cake.

Pier Head, Gorleston-on-Sea

Fried Guinea Fowl

Originally a game bird, guinea fowl are now farmed as poultry.
They are in best condition between February and June.

1 large guinea fowl, about 3 lb., cleaned and jointed   2 oz. butter
1 large onion, peeled and finely chopped or minced
3 oz. streaky bacon, chopped   ¼ lb button mushrooms, wiped
¼ pint dry white wine   Salt and black pepper
Watercress to garnish

Joint the guinea fowl, place in a saucepan and cover with water. Bring to the boil, cover and simmer for about 1 hour, skimming once or twice. Remove the joints from the pan, strain the stock and boil the liquid hard to reduce to about a ¼ pint. Meanwhile, dust the joints with seasoned flour. Melt the butter in a frying pan and gently fry the joints until lightly brown. Remove and keep hot. Put the onion in the pan and fry until soft and transparent, adding more butter if necessary, then add the bacon and fry, stirring, until lightly crisp. Add the mushrooms and fry, stirring, for a further minute. Pour in the wine and the reduced stock and bring to the boil, stirring. Return the guinea fowl joints to the pan, cover and simmer for 5 minutes, seasoning to taste. Remove the joints and place on a warm serving dish. Spoon the sauce over them, and serve garnished with watercress. Serves 3 to 4.

Baked Apple Dumplings

Whole apples with a spicy filling, baked in a pastry envelope. This traditional farmhouse pudding was often served at Victorian shooting party lunches.

8 oz. shortcrust pastry   1-2 oz. sultanas or raisins
4 small cooking apples, peeled and cored   Pinch of ground cinnamon
1 oz. butter, softened   Pinch of ground cloves
1 oz. soft brown sugar   Beaten egg or milk to glaze

Set oven to 400°F or Mark 6. Roll out the pastry on a floured surface and cut into circles or squares each big enough to enclose an apple completely. Place an apple in the centre of each piece of pastry. Mix together the butter, sugar, sultanas or raisins and spices, and fill the centres of the apples with the mixture. Enclose each apple completely with the pastry, sealing well, then turn the dumplings upside down on a greased baking sheet, so that the joins are underneath. Glaze the dumplings with beaten egg or milk and bake for 30 minutes until the pastry is golden. While still hot, sprinkle with a little caster sugar. Serve hot or cold with cream or custard.

Dressed Crab

Cromer crabs are renowned throughout Norfolk. A crab should feel heavy for its size and one medium size shellfish, about 3 lb, will make a meal for two persons..

2 medium-size crabs, boiled
3-4 oz. fresh white breadcrumbs
Salt and pepper
Lemon juice
1 tablespoon salad oil
2 tablespoons white wine vinegar

GARNISH

2 hard-boiled eggs Chopped parsley

First remove the brown meat from the shells and the white meat from the large claws, and clean the shells thoroughly. Mix the dark meat with the breadcrumbs, season with salt and pepper and add lemon juice to taste. Arrange the mixture inside the shells at the short ends. Flake the white meat, mix with oil and vinegar, season and arrange in the centre of the shells. Garnish with sieved hard-boiled egg yolks, chopped egg whites and parsley. Serve with brown bread-and-butter and a green salad. Serves 4.

Cromer from the beach

Vinegar Cake

A light farmhouse fruit cake that keeps well. Being eggless it was usually made when the hens were off lay.

8 oz. butter 1 lb. plain flour 8 oz. sugar
8 oz. raisins 8 oz. sultanas
8 fl.oz. milk 2 tablespoons cider vinegar
1 teaspoon bicarbonate of soda, blended with 1 tablespoon milk

Set oven to 350°F or Mark 4. Grease and line a 9 inch round cake tin. In a bowl, rub the butter into the flour until the mixture resembles breadcrumbs, then stir in the sugar and the raisins and sultanas. Pour the milk into a large jug and add the cider vinegar, then stir in the bicarbonate of soda (the mixture will froth up). Add the liquid to the cake mixture and stir well. Turn into the cake tin and bake for 30 minutes. Then reduce oven to 300°F or Mark 2 and bake for a further 1 to 1¼ hours or until a skewer inserted into the cake comes out clean. If the cake appears to be browning too quickly on top during cooking, cover lightly with a piece of greaseproof paper. When cooked, allow the cake to cool in the tin before turning out on to a wire rack.

Dressmaker Tripe

The whimsical name for this dish probably comes from the fact that the tripe is sewn up to contain the filling.

2 lb. tripe
½ lb. small onions, peeled
8 oz. fresh white breadcrumbs
1 heaped tablespoon chopped parsley
½ teaspoon chopped thyme
1 teaspoon grated lemon rind
Salt and black pepper
1 large egg, beaten
6 to 8 rashers of streaky bacon

Set oven to 350°F or Mark 4. Butter a large ovenproof dish. Boil the onions in lightly salted water until soft. Cool slightly and chop finely. In a bowl, mix together the onion with the breadcrumbs, herbs, lemon rind and seasoning and bind together with beaten egg. Spread out the tripe, smooth side uppermost and season lightly. Then spread the filling mixture over half the tripe. Fold the other half over and sew up the edges neatly to form a parcel. Put the tripe in the dish and cover with the bacon rashers. Bake for 30 minutes, then drain off the liquid that has accumulated in the dish, leaving just enough to prevent the tripe from sticking. Bake for a further 30 minutes, covering with kitchen foil if necessary. Serve with a rich, brown gravy accompanied by plain boiled potatoes and green peas. Serves 4 to 6.

Norfolk Apple Pie

An old-fashioned apple pie flavoured with orange marmalade.

12 oz. shortcrust pastry
2 lb. cooking apples
1 dessertspoon lemon juice
1 oz. butter
1 tablespoon sugar
2 tablespoons orange marmalade
2 oz. currants or sultanas
Beaten egg or milk to glaze

Set oven to 400°F or Mark 6. Grease a deep 8 inch pie plate. Roll out the pastry on a lightly floured surface and use half to line the pie plate. Peel, core and slice the apples, and pour the lemon juice over. Melt the butter in a saucepan, add the apples and cook until soft, stirring frequently to prevent them sticking. Add the sugar, then beat the apples to a pulp (a potato masher is ideal for this). Place half of the apple mixture in the pie plate, smooth the marmalade over and sprinkle on the currants or sultanas; top with the remaining apple. Use the remaining pastry as a lid, sealing the edges well. Trim and use any left-over pastry to make leaves and apples to decorate. Glaze the pie with beaten egg or milk and bake for 15 minutes. Then reduce oven to 350°F or Mark 4 and bake for a further 15 to 20 minutes, or until the pie is golden. Serves 4.

The Sands, Great Yarmouth

Harvest Loaves

These flat loaves were traditionally served to harvesters working in the fields.

1 lb. self-raising flour
Pinch of salt
½ teaspoon ground nutmeg
4 oz. lard
4 oz. butter or margarine
1 oz. sugar
2 oz. currants or sultanas
2 eggs, beaten
Milk
A little extra sugar

Set oven to 375°F or Mark 5. In a bowl, mix together the flour, salt and nutmeg. Rub in the fats until the mixture resembles breadcrumbs, then stir in the sugar and dried fruit. Add the eggs and sufficient milk to form a soft dough. Turn out on to a floured surface, knead lightly, then form into rounds, each about the size of a saucer. Place on a greased baking sheet, leaving a space between, brush with a little milk and sprinkle a little sugar over. Mark the top of each loaf with a diamond pattern and bake for 25 to 30 minutes or until golden. Makes about 4 loaves.

Rabbit in the Dairy

A popular farmhouse method of cooking rabbit that gives it a delicate, almost chicken flavour. The 'dairy' refers to the milk in which the rabbit is cooked.

8 rabbit joints Seasoned flour
3 rashers unsmoked back bacon, chopped
1 small onion, finely chopped 2 sprigs parsley
Salt and black pepper
½ pint milk ¼ oz. cornflour
Chopped fresh parsley to garnish

Set oven to 325°F or Mark 3. Dust the rabbit joints with a little seasoned flour and place in an ovenproof casserole with the bacon, onion, parsley and seasoning. Bring the milk to the boil and pour over. Cover and cook for 2 hours or until the rabbit is tender. Remove the rabbit joints to a warm serving dish and keep hot. Discard the parsley and pour the milk mixture into a saucepan, adding a little extra milk if necessary. Blend the cornflour with a little cold water, then stir into the milk. Bring to the boil and stir until the sauce has thickened a little. Pour the sauce over the rabbit and serve garnished with chopped parsley, and accompanied by carrots and boiled potatoes. Serves 4.

Norfolk Plough Pudding

This pudding was traditionally served on Plough Monday, the first Monday after Twelfth Day when, by tradition, spring ploughing was due to begin following the Christmas holiday.

8 oz. self-raising flour
A good pinch of salt
3 oz. shredded suet
1 lb. pork sausagemeat
8 rashers streaky bacon, chopped
1 large onion, peeled and chopped
1 teaspoon chopped sage
½ oz. brown sugar
Water or pork stock

Grease a 2 pint pudding basin. In a bowl, mix the flour, salt and suet together then add sufficient cold water to form a soft dough. Turn out on to a lightly floured surface and roll out. Use ⅔ of the dough to line the pudding basin, reserving the remaining ⅓ for the lid. Seal any gaps well, and use the sausagemeat to line the dough, pressing them well together. Mix the bacon, onion, sage and sugar together and put in the basin, adding sufficient water or stock just to cover. Cover with a dough lid, press the edges firmly together, and seal with a little water. Cover the top with a circle of greaseproof paper and finally cover securely with kitchen foil. Steam for 3½ to 4 hours. Serve with boiled potatoes and a selection of vegetables, and thick brown gravy served separately. Serves 4 to 6.

Baked Bloaters

A supper dish from Great Yarmouth where traditionally the bloaters were baked between two tin plates.

1 bloater per person 1 oz. butter
¼ teaspoon dry mustard powder
1 heaped teaspoon finely chopped onion

Set oven to 350°F or Mark 4. Wash the bloater, dry on kitchen paper, then cut off the head and tail. Slit open and remove the backbone, using a sharp knife. Spread the inside of the bloater with butter and close up. Place in a buttered, ovenproof dish and sprinkle with the mustard and chopped onion. Cover with a piece of kitchen foil and bake for 15 to 20 minutes or until the bloater is soft. Do not overcook or it will dry out. Serve topped with a pat of butter and accompanied by crusty bread.

Fish Soup

Traditionally this recipe included a cod's head, a popular ingredient in the 19th century.

2 lb. mixed white fish   1 onion, peeled and chopped
1 leek, washed, trimmed and cut into rings
1 stick celery, washed, trimmed and chopped
2 tablespoons tomato purée   4 fl.oz. white wine
A 'walnut' of butter   2 tablespoons flour   ¼ pint milk
A little grated lemon rind   1 teaspoon chopped fennel leaves
2 tablespoons chopped parsley   Salt and black pepper

Put the fish, onion, leek and celery in a saucepan and cover with 2 pints of water. Bring to the boil and simmer until the fish is cooked. Lift out the fish and flake coarsely, removing any skin and bones. Return the skin and bones to the saucepan with the vegetables and continue to cook for a further 20 minutes, adding more water if necessary, then strain and pour the liquid into a clean saucepan. Stir in the tomato purée and the white wine. Melt the butter in a small saucepan and stir in the flour, then gradually add the milk, stirring until smooth. Add to the fish liquid and cook for 3 to 4 minutes, stirring all the time. Add the flaked fish, lemon rind and chopped herbs and season to taste. Bring to the boil, stirring lightly, and serve at once, garnished with a little extra chopped herbs, if desired.

Game Pie

Pheasant or partridge, steak and bacon form the basis of this substantial pie.

1 pheasant or a brace of partridge, cleaned and jointed
8 oz. stewing steak, cut into 1 inch cubes   Seasoned flour
2 rashers streaky bacon, cut into strips   1 oz. butter
1 onion, peeled and chopped   1 oz. button mushrooms, wiped
A bouquet garni   Salt and black pepper   1 pint prepared brown stock
10 oz. shortcrust pastry or flaky pastry   1 egg, beaten

Set oven to 300°F or Mark 2. Melt the butter in a pan and fry the onion until just soft; remove and set aside. Dust the steak with seasoned flour, brown lightly in the pan and place in the bottom of a deep pie dish. Repeat with the pheasant or partridge joints, place them on top of the meat, then scatter over the onion, bacon strips and mushrooms. Add the herbs and season to taste. Pour on sufficient stock to cover, cover with kitchen foil and cook for 1½ to 2 hours. Remove from the oven and allow to cool. Increase oven to 400°F or Mark 6. Remove the herbs and discard, then add sufficient stock to bring the level to about ½ inch from the top of the filling. Roll out the pastry on a lightly floured surface, cover the pie and trim. Decorate the top and brush with beaten egg. Bake for 20 minutes, then reduce oven to 300°F or Mark 2 and bake for a further 15 minutes or until the pie is golden. Serves 4 to 6.

Hen-on-Her-Nest

A useful recipe when faced with preparing an older chicken.

1 boiling fowl, 3 to 4 lb. 2 carrots, peeled and sliced 1 onion, peeled and sliced
2 sticks celery, washed and sliced A bouquet garni
6 whole black peppercorns ½ teaspoon ground ginger ½ teaspoon ground mace
¾ to 1 pint water or chicken stock 3 oz. butter 4 to 8 eggs, hard-boiled
12 oz. long grain rice 2 oz. plain flour ¼ pint double cream
Salt and black pepper Parsley sprigs to garnish

Put the chicken in a large saucepan with the vegetables, herbs and spices. Almost cover with water or stock, season, bring to the boil, cover and simmer for 2 to 2½ hours. Set oven to 350°F or Mark 4. Remove the chicken and drain well, reserving the stock. Place in a roasting tin, spread 1 oz butter over the breast and legs and cook in the oven for 10 minutes to brown the skin. Hard-boil the eggs and cook the rice in 1½ pints salted water. Melt the remaining 2 oz butter in a pan and stir in the flour. Remove from the heat and gradually stir in ¼ pint stock. Heat gently, stirring, until the sauce thickens. Add the cream and season. Shell the hard-boiled eggs. Drain the rice well and arrange around the edge of a large serving dish. Put the chicken 'on her nest' and tuck the eggs around and beneath it. Heat the sauce (do not boil), pour a little around the chicken and the remainder into a sauceboat. Garnish with parsley.

Plaice Cooked in Cream

A simple and delicate way to cook plaice fillets.

8 single plaice fillets, skinned
½ oz. butter
1 small onion, peeled and chopped
5 fl.oz. double cream
¼ pint fish stock
Salt and black pepper
Parsley sprigs to garnish

Melt the butter in a large frying pan. Add the onion and cook until softened but not brown. Stir in the cream and the stock and heat through, stirring constantly. Season to taste. Lay the plaice fillets in the pan and spoon a little of the liquid over them. Cover and poach for 5 to 6 minutes or until the fish is tender and cooked through. Transfer the plaice fillets to a warm serving dish. Continue to cook the liquid for a little longer until it thickens slightly, then spoon over the fish. Serve, garnished with parsley sprigs. Serves 4.

Rabbit Casserole with Herb Dumplings

A well-flavoured dish which makes a good standby in cold weather.

8 rabbit joints Seasoned flour 8 rashers streaky bacon, chopped
1 onion, peeled and chopped 2 sticks celery, washed, trimmed and chopped
2 carrots, peeled and sliced A bouquet garni
1 pint chicken stock Salt and black pepper

HERB DUMPLINGS

3 oz. self-raising flour Pinch of salt Pinch of dry mustard powder
1½ oz. shredded suet 1 dessertspoon snipped chives 1 tablespoon chopped parsley

Set oven to 325°F or Mark 3. Fry the bacon lightly and place in a casserole dish. Dust the rabbit joints with seasoned flour and brown lightly on all sides. Place the onion, celery and carrots in the casserole and put the rabbit joints on top. Add the herbs. Pour the stock into the frying pan and bring to the boil, stirring. Season, then pour into the casserole. Cover and cook for about 1½ to 2 hours or until the rabbit joints are tender. Herb Dumplings: mix the flour, salt, mustard powder, suet and herbs together in a bowl and add sufficient cold water to form a soft dough. Form into 12 balls and place in the casserole, about 30 minutes before the end of the cooking time. Cover and cook until the dumplings are well risen. Serve with boiled potatoes and runner beans. Serves 4.

Fruit Chutney

A preserve made with a mixture of plums, apples, tomatoes and onions.

1 lb. plums, stoned
1 lb. cooking apples, peeled and cored
1 lb. tomatoes, peeled
2 large onions, peeled
1 clove garlic, peeled
1-1½ teaspoons salt
A good pinch cayenne pepper
½ teaspoon mixed spice
½ teaspoon ground mace
½ teaspoon ground ginger
½ lb. sultanas
1 pint vinegar
½ lb. brown sugar

Mince or finely chop the fruit and vegetables. Put in a preserving pan and add the salt, spices, sultanas and vinegar. Bring to the boil and simmer, stirring from time to time to prevent sticking, until the mixture is thick and tender. Add the sugar and stir until dissolved, then bring back to the boil and simmer for about 2 hours, or until the chutney has thickened and all excess liquid has evaporated. Cool slightly, then pot in clean, warm jars. Cover when cool with non-metallic lids. Serve with cold meats or cheese. Makes about 4 lb. of chutney.

Norfolk Gingers

These old-fashioned ginger biscuits include mixed spice in the ingredients.

8 oz. plain flour
4 oz. brown sugar
2 teaspoons ground ginger
½ teaspoon mixed spice
4 oz. butter
A scant teaspoon bicarbonate of soda
2 tablespoons warm milk
1 egg

Set oven to 350°F or Mark 4. In a bowl, mix the flour, sugar and spices together, then rub in the butter. Dissolve the bicarbonate of soda in the warm milk, then add the egg and beat together. Stir into the dry ingredients and knead the mixture until smooth. Flour the hands lightly and divide the mixture into small, equal size balls. Place these, well apart, on a greased baking sheet and flatten each ball slightly. Bake for 20 to 25 minutes and leave on the baking sheet until cool. If desired each biscuit can be decorated with a small piece of crystallised ginger before baking.

Mussel Pudding

An economical fisherman's dish. When preparing the mussels, scrub them thoroughly and discard any that do not close up when lightly tapped.

40 to 50 mussels, thoroughly scrubbed with 'beards' removed
3 oz. plain flour   1 teaspoon baking powder
3 oz. shredded suet   Pinch of salt
1 small onion, finely chopped
4 rashers streaky bacon, finely chopped
Salt and pepper
1 tablespoon chopped parsley

Put the mussels in a single layer in a thick-based pan with 2 to 3 tablespoons of water. Cover and heat for a few minutes. The mussels will open and can be spooned from the shells. Repeat if necessary. In a bowl, mix the flour, baking powder, suet and salt together, then add sufficient cold water to form a firm dough. Spread the mussels, onion, bacon and parsley on to the dough and season to taste. Roll up like a Swiss Roll and damp the ends to seal. Wrap lightly in greaseproof paper or kitchen foil, and then tie up in a cloth. Boil or steam in a covered pan for 2 hours. If desired, before serving, the Mussel Pudding can be placed on an ovenproof serving dish and put in a hot oven for a few minutes to crisp the surface. Serve sprinkled with chopped parsley.

The Colonnade Shelters, Hunstanton

Sweet Omelette

Sometimes called Prior's Omelette, this recipe was popular in church circles.

1 small orange
1 tablespoon double cream
1 dessertspoon honey
2 eggs, separated
A 'walnut' of butter

Grate the rind from half the orange, then cut the orange in half and set aside the rind and the ungrated half. Squeeze the juice from the grated half. Whip the cream lightly, then fold in the orange juice and the honey. Set aside in the refrigerator. Separate the eggs, whisking the whites until they stand in soft peaks. Beat the yolks. Melt the butter in an omelette pan. Fold the egg yolks into the egg whites and, when the butter is sizzling, pour the mixture into the pan. Cook for 2 minutes, turning the edges of the omelette away from the side of the pan as it cooks. Spoon the cream mixture on to half the omelette and fold the other half over. Carefully transfer to a warm plate and serve at once, sprinkled with orange rind and accompanied by the remaining orange, cut into segments. Serves 1.

Honey-roasted Turkey

The butter/honey mixture gives the turkey meat a delicious flavour and adds a rich, dark 'crust' to the skin. Allow approximately 15 minutes roasting time to each 1 lb in weight of turkey.

1 oven-ready turkey, 8 to 10 lb.
1 small apple, peeled
1 small onion, peeled
1 small potato, peeled
Salt and black pepper
A thick slice of lemon
3 oz. butter
6 oz. thick honey

Put inside the turkey the apple, onion and potato (they will help to keep the turkey meat moist) and season lightly. Place the turkey in a roasting tin and rub the skin lightly with the lemon. Melt the butter and honey together in a pan, stirring, and pour the mixture over the turkey. Allow to stand for about 30 to 40 minutes, spooning over the butter/honey mixture frequently. Set oven to 400°F or Mark 6. Roast the turkey for 30 minutes, basting from time to time. Reduce oven to 350°F or Mark 4 and roast for a further 30 minutes, basting from time to time. Cover with kitchen foil and continue cooking until the turkey is cooked. For the last 15 minutes of cooking time remove the foil to crisp the skin. Serve with roast potatoes and seasonal vegetables and with a thin gravy made from the giblets. Serves 6 to 8.

Norfolk Syllabub

This is sometimes called 'Everlasting' syllabub because, when made, it will 'hold its shape' for about 12 hours.

¼ pint white wine
1 tablespoon medium sherry
2 tablespoons brandy
1 lemon
2 oz. caster sugar
½ pint double cream

Pour the wine, sherry and brandy into a bowl. Peel the lemon very thinly and squeeze out the juice. Add the peel and juice to the wine mixture, cover and leave in a cool place overnight. Next day, remove the peel and discard. Add the sugar to the wine mixture, stirring until it has dissolved. Pour in the cream and whip until the mixture stands in soft peaks. Spoon into four tall glasses or sundae dishes and serve with boudoir or cat's tongue biscuits. Serves 4.

Norfolk Fair Buttons

These Button Biscuits were traditionally sold as fairings at fairs throughout the county and particularly around the town of Diss.

8 oz. plain flour
4 oz. soft brown sugar
¼ oz. ground ginger
Pinch of bicarbonate of soda
2 oz. lard
4 oz. golden syrup

Set oven to 350°F or Mark 4. In a bowl, mix together the flour, sugar, ginger and bicarbonate of soda and rub in the lard until the mixture resembles breadcrumbs. Add the syrup and mix together thoroughly. Roll out thinly on a lightly floured surface and cut into 2 inch rounds with a pastry cutter. Place on a greased baking sheet and cook for 10 to 12 minutes. Cool on a wire rack.

The Charter

A delicious dinner party dessert; a favourite of the 18th century cleric and diarist, Parson Woodforde.

1 pint whipping cream
2 eggs plus 2 egg yolks
1 lemon
18 'no soak' apricot halves
3 tablespoons sugar

Peel the rind off the lemon very thinly and stir into the cream. Cover and leave in a cool place overnight. Next day, set oven to 300°F or Mark 2. In a bowl, beat the eggs and egg yolks together. Remove the lemon rind from the cream, and pour the cream over the beaten eggs. Combine together, adding a little sugar to sweeten, if necessary. Divide the mixture between 6 ramekins. Cover each with kitchen foil, place in a *bain marie* and cook for 25 minutes, until the mixture is set but still creamy. Remove the foil and allow the mixture to cool. Meanwhile, place the apricots in a saucepan with sufficient water to cover, bring to the boil, cover and simmer until tender. Add the sugar and 1 teaspoon of lemon juice and boil until the apricots are well glazed and the liquid has vanished. Shake the pan regularly to avoid burning. Place an apricot on top of each ramekin and serve.

METRIC CONVERSIONS

The weights, measures and oven temperatures used in the preceding recipes can be easily converted to their metric equivalents. The conversions listed below are only approximate, having been rounded up or down as may be appropriate.

Weights

Avoirdupois	Metric
1 oz.	just under 30 grams
4 oz. (¼ lb.)	app. 115 grams
8 oz. (½ lb.)	app. 230 grams
1 lb.	454 grams

Liquid Measures

Imperial	Metric
1 tablespoon (liquid only)	20 millilitres
1 fl. oz.	app. 30 millilitres
1 gill (¼ pt.)	app. 145 millilitres
½ pt.	app. 285 millilitres
1 pt.	app. 570 millilitres
1 qt.	app. 1.140 litres

Oven Temperatures

	°Fahrenheit	Gas Mark	°Celsius
Slow	300	2	150
	325	3	170
Moderate	350	4	180
	375	5	190
	400	6	200
Hot	425	7	220
	450	8	230
	475	9	240

Flour as specified in these recipes refers to plain flour unless otherwise described.